FRAGMENTS OF NIGHTMARE

Ngo Binh Anh Khoa

Fragments of Nightmare

First Printing

ISBN 978-1-970860-02-3

Cover Art Credit: Katsushika Hokusai. Sarayashiki (The House of Broken Plates), from the series "One Hundred Ghost Tales (Hyaku monogatari)," 1931-1932. The Smithsonian National Museum of Asian Art Collection.

CUTTLEFISH
BOOKS

ACKNOWLEDGEMENTS

Grateful appreciation is offered to the editors and publishers of *Otoroshi Journal*, *Scifaikuest*, *SPOOKY Magazine*, and *Star*Line* in which some of these poems have previously appeared or are forthcoming.

To my parents,
for their unwavering support
for my life choices and interests

FRAGMENTS OF NIGHTMARE

Murderous Temptations

heirloom
a patchwork quilt
of human flesh

out of red paint
the artist puts on his coat
dagger in his pocket

home alone
the sounds of footsteps
up on the attic

home alone
the sounds of footsteps
circling my bed

amaryllis
the shade of red spreading
across her slit neck

Valentine's Day
a bouquet of roses
soaked with blood

blind date
new set of eyeballs
for my collection

clouded moon
the man in the alley pockets
his victim's eyes

change of season
fallen leaves dyed red
a dismembered corpse

crescent moon
maggots wriggling around in
a slashed throat

grocery run
beside a cabbage's head
a human's

birthday party
the laughter of the clown
no-one invited

dumpster diving
the bits and pieces to sate
the cannibal's hunger

circling vulture
the hooded figure
of a stalker

fresh cattle feed
yet another poster
of a missing person

Spectral Chains

autopsy table
I look down
at my corpse

autopsy report
I find out the cause
of my death

cheap real estate
the agent never mentioned
the ghosts that linger

Day of the Dead
I receive a phone call
from my late mother

moonlit graveyard
the weeping angels
break the silence

ghost month
the midnight train
moans toward the moon

ghost marriage
a brush of cold air
against my lips

selfies with new friends
their faces do not appear
in any photo

winter wind
a whisper of my name in
an empty graveyard

winter cold
waking up next to a doll
I never brought to bed

New Year countdown
the dusty planchette moves
3...2...1

gym's locker room
my reflection winks at me
all on its own

morning mist
outside the penthouse's window
half-faded handprints

new moon
our late grandma's rocking chair
begins to creak

lunar eclipse
the sleepwalker tightens
his own noose

From out the Restless Graves

teary-eyed jester
underneath a guillotine
laughing his head off

nightly tryst
at the cemetery
undead lover

breastfeeding
against her bosom
a swaddled corpse

our baby's first cry
the gift of life from
the necromancer

graveyard shift
the dead stare
in silence

midnight
my wife lying in my bed
instead of her grave

blood moon
in the side-view mirror
the roadkill's glare

wilted sunflower
the sound of my voice
fills this coffin

autumn chill
a mad scientist harvests
a corpse's organs

red spider lilies
a stained lab coat
littered with bite marks

winter storm
two corpses fighting
over a roadkill

epidemic
a crow perching on
a zombie's head

muscle memory
zombies roam, eyes fixed
on dead smartphones

old habits die hard
my reanimated dog
wags its tail at me

old habits die hard
my reanimated dog
wags its tail at me

Hunters in the Dark

blood moon
a dripping wet eyeball in
a raven's beak

clouded moon
a raven's carcass in
the scarecrow's grip

harvest moon
the scarecrow's grin
grows wider

harvest season
one more head
in the scarecrow's basket

hunter's moon
a gargoyle's gone missing
from the church's steeple

"Am I a real boy?"
asks the puppet wearing
a pauper's flayed skin

tracks on the soil
footprints turning into
paw prints

blood moon
a silhouette of a bat
into a man

All Hallows' Eve
a carved pumpkin for a head
not a costume

trick or treat
a peeled apple
a skinless corpse

suicide forest
the murmurings
among the trees

winter dawn
a trail of entrails
stains the snow

abandoned farm
a spider swallows
a human skull

half moon
a voice from the ocean
in the sailors' ears

full moon
a sudden howl from
the nursing home

ABOUT THE AUTHOR

Ngo Binh Anh Khoa is a teacher of English in Ho Chi Minh City, Vietnam. In his free time, he enjoys reading fiction and writing speculative stories and poetry. His works have previously appeared in Heroic Fantasy Quarterly, Star*Line, Weirdbook, Spectral Realms, and elsewhere. He also enjoys writing haiku, some of which have received awards and honorable mentions in international contests in the US, Japan, Canada, and a few other countries.

www.ingramcontent.com/pod-product-compliance
Lightning Source LLC
Chambersburg PA
CBHW041629140626
46547CB00031B/1630